EXPLORING
tree
habitats

Written by Patti Seifert
Wildlife illustrations by Peg Doherty
Cartoon illustrations by Miriam Katin

MONDO

Gibbon   page 21

Long-nosed bat   page 12

Animal life in a baobab tree   page 17

Linsang   page 20

Bald eagle   page 5

Black-tailed deer   page 4

Contents

Sitka spruce

Alaska, U.S.A.
California, U.S.A.
Pacific Ocean

The Sitka spruce grows along the Pacific Coast from the middle of California to southern Alaska. The Sitka's needle-shaped leaves and shallow root system help it survive long dry periods.

Pollen dust is in the spores of the spruce cones. The wind blows the dust to the female cones of nearby trees and pollinates them.

female cone (seed)

male cone (pollen)

leaf

shallow roots

3

red-tailed hawk

stellar jay

The tree mouse spends its whole life in the tree.

By hanging upside down, the red-breasted nut hatch easily finds insects on the underside of branches.

black-tailed deer at rest

fallen needles

A porcupine can damage the tree if it eats too much bark.

northern toad

4

A bald eagle roosts in the Sitka spruce. It eats fish from the nearby stream.

Seeds stored by a deer mouse can germinate even after several years.

The deer mouse stores conifer seeds. Some may grow into new trees.

mushrooms

A shrew mole looks for earthworms in the wet ground under the tree.

ptarmagin

Germination

The Sitka spruce grows from a seed that drops from a mature tree onto the soil. Each tree produces many seeds. But some never reach the ground because animals eat them first.

1. Seeds drop from the parent tree and animals scatter them.

2. A forgotten seed can wait for several years to germinate, or sprout.

3. When the conditions are right, seeds put down roots.

4. The young tree needs an open space with light to grow.

HAPPY 5TH BIRTHDAY SPRUCE!

A Sitka spruce can live for 850 years. It can grow to be 280 feet tall and 25 to 47 feet in circumference above the buttresses.

CAN YOU FIND IT?

Turn back the page and find the hawk moth.

White oak

The white oak tree grows in forests and yards throughout the eastern part of the United States. Its roots can store an abundance of food, which helps the tree adapt to harsh seasonal changes.

fruit-acorn

The oak's thick trunk protects it from lightning bolts. The roots look like a mirror image of the tree above.

leaf

trunk

flower

branching roots

At dawn, a red squirrel scurries along the branches nibbling leaf buds.

A pileated (*pil-ee-ate-id*) woodpecker searches for insects in the bark of the tree.

An adult white oak can produce 750 acorns a year. Two or three of these may become an adult tree. The rest are usually eaten by animals and insects.

turkey cock

A fox family has dug a den at the base of the tree.

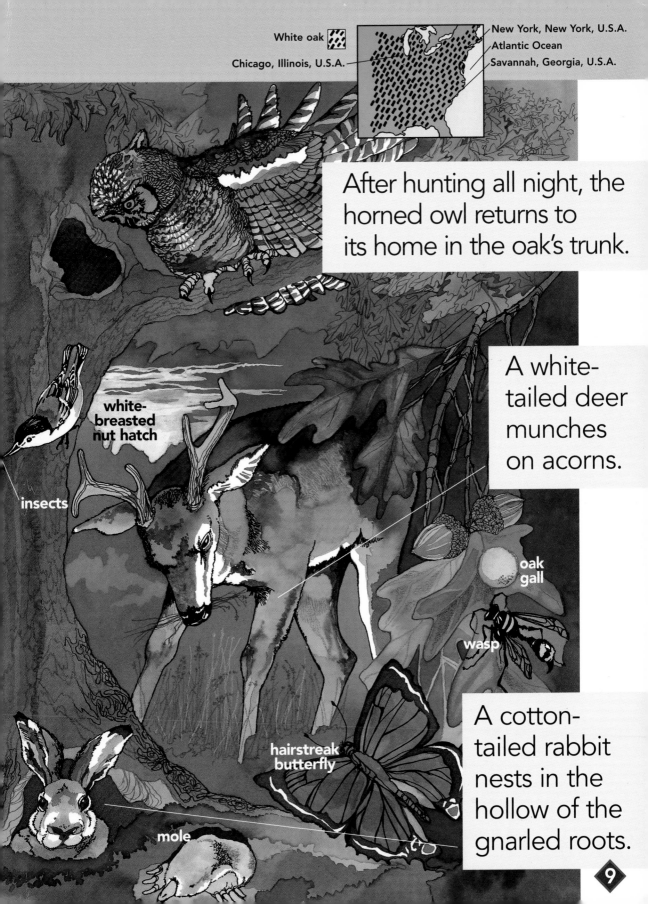

White oak

New York, New York, U.S.A.
Atlantic Ocean
Savannah, Georgia, U.S.A.
Chicago, Illinois, U.S.A.

After hunting all night, the horned owl returns to its home in the oak's trunk.

white-breasted nut hatch

insects

A white-tailed deer munches on acorns.

oak gall

wasp

hairstreak butterfly

A cotton-tailed rabbit nests in the hollow of the gnarled roots.

mole

The oak begins to bear acorns after it is 20 years old. Acorns are oak seeds and can grow into new trees.

1. A tree may drop as many as 750 acorns a year.

2. Animals like this squirrel eat or store most of a tree's acorns. But sometimes an animal will forget or lose one.

3. An abandoned acorn puts out roots before the weather turns cold.

4. Only two or three acorns will actually become trees.

GEORGE WASHINGTON LEANED HERE 1776

A white oak can live for 300 years. It can grow to be 87 feet tall and 25 ½ feet in circumference.

10

CAN YOU FIND IT?

Turn back the page and find the walking stick.

Saguaro

The saguaro (*sa-wah-ro*) grows in the Sonora Desert. The saguaro's shallow roots soak up rain as soon as it falls, and the tree's waxy skin allows little moisture to escape.

waxy skin

no leaves

Saguaro flowers open at night and close the next afternoon. The tree's skin has accordion pleats that expand when it is full of water.

spines protect skin

flower

fruit

shallow roots

night/flower

Harris hawk

The white-winged dove rests at night after carrying pollen from flower to flower throughout the day.

An elf owl moves into a gila woodpecker's abandoned nest.

The long-nosed bat uses its long tongue to feed on nectar and pollen from the flower.

The saguaro's wooden spinal system helps keep it stable. Native Americans used this wood for building material.

day/fruit

A gila woodpecker taps a new nest into the saguaro's trunk.

A coyote visits the cactus looking for fruit to eat but finds a desert mouse instead.

Javelina pigs munch the juicy red fruit that has fallen to the ground.

collared lizard

13

Germination

The saguaro begins to bear fruit after it is 50 years old. A few of the seeds inside the fruit will grow into a new tree.

1. The ripe fruit attracts animals such as the desert mouse. It eats the fruit, collecting seeds on its whiskers.

2. The seeds travel with the desert mouse. Other animals and rain can move seeds also.

3. Most of the seeds are eaten or parched by the hot sun. But protected seeds put down roots when it rains and grow into seedlings.

4. Saguaro seedlings are food for many animals. Very few are left alone to grow into giant cacti.

CAN YOU FIND IT?

A saguaro grows very slowly. It takes one year to grow 1 inch tall and nine years to grow 6 inches. By the time the saguaro is one hundred years old, it can be 50 feet tall.

Turn back the page and find the gecko.

Baobab

Africa — Indian Ocean — Madagascar

The baobab grows on the dry savannas of Africa. It adapts to the dry environment by storing water in its roots and trunk. Elephants often gouge the baobab's trunk looking for water in the long dry season.

Baobabs do not bear leaves, flowers, or fruit for most of the year, but their leaves and flowers bloom twice during the rainy season.

flower

leaf

fruit

trunk scar from elephant

African elephant

shallow roots

night/flower

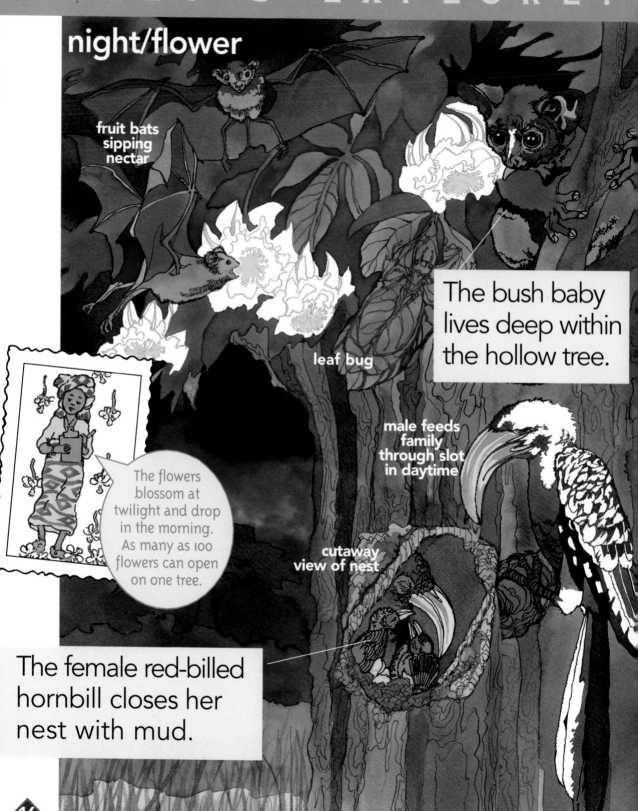

fruit bats sipping nectar

leaf bug

The bush baby lives deep within the hollow tree.

male feeds family through slot in daytime

The flowers blossom at twilight and drop in the morning. As many as 100 flowers can open on one tree.

cutaway view of nest

The female red-billed hornbill closes her nest with mud.

day/fruit

Baobab

Lake Victoria
Mombasa, Kenya
Madagascar

long-horned beetle

lilac-breasted roller

A green tree snake heads for a buffalo weaver's nest.

The red-billed buffalo weaver takes months to build its nest with thorny branches.

A baboon breaks open and eats the hard fruit called monkey bread.

Germination

Baobabs grow from the seeds of the fruit. The fruit must be cracked open by an animal so the seeds can drop to the soil and sprout.

1. To eat the fruit, a baboon breaks the fruit open, exposing its seeds.

2. The seeds fall out of the fruit.

3. The seeds lay dormant during the dry season, which lasts for many weeks.

4. The seeds put down roots after the heavy rains soak them.

The baobab is one of the oldest living trees in the world. It can live to be 2,000 years old, and its trunk is larger than any other tree's.

CAN YOU FIND IT?

Turn back the page and find the bark mantis.

Durian

Thailand · Borneo · Indonesia · Pacific Ocean

The durian is found in the rain forests of Southeast Asia. Its roots are shallow, so as the tree grows larger the trunk develops buttresses for balance. A large number of pollinators are attracted to the durian's flowers, so the tree bears a lot of fruit.

flower

fruit

leaf

buttresses

Asian elephant

The fruit of the durian smells like sour milk. But it is eaten by many animals and is considered a delicacy by humans.

shallow roots

night/flower

Bats move from tree to tree feeding on nectar and pollinating the flowers.

flying fox bat

cave nectar bats

tree shrew

A linsang waits to pounce on a sleeping sunbird.

The durian can produce thousands of flowers that fill the air with an aroma so strong it attracts bats from great distances.

The sunbird rests after an active day of moving from flower to flower.

day/fruit

Durian
Thailand
Malaysia
Borneo
Indonesia

A Prevost's squirrel searches for insects on the leaves and fruit.

The Asian elephant is one of the many animals that likes the taste of the durian's fruit.

gibbon

long-horned beetle

The moonrat eats rotting fruit covered with insects.

Durians grow from seeds encased in fruit. The growth of a new tree depends on animals to open the fruit and eat the seeds or let them fall to the ground.

1. The fruit can weigh 5 pounds. It drops when it is ripe.

2. Animals such as elephants eat the fruit. Some seeds are eaten with the fruit and others drop to the ground.

3. Seeds are also dispersed in the elephant's droppings, probably some distance from the parent tree.

4. A seed sprouts, fertilized by the elephant's manure.

A durian can live for 250 years. It can grow to be 160 feet tall and 19 feet in circumference.

CAN YOU FIND IT?

Turn back the page and find the leaf mimic.

Glossary

abandoned - left behind; no longer used or lived in.

adapt - to change in order to survive in a different environment.

buttress - a spreading, fanlike growth at the base of a tree trunk. It helps support the tree.

circumference - the outer line around a circle and the rim around the trunk of a tree.

conifer - a tree that has cones, usually an evergreen.

delicacy - a tasty treat that is not easy to get.

disperse - to move or scatter in a different direction.

dormant - completely inactive; a sleep-like state.

fertilize - to add material to the soil which helps plants grow better.

gnarled - thick and twisted.

germinate - to begin to grow with the help of moisture and warmth.

gouge - to cut or scoop out a hole.

habitat - the place where a plant or animal lives.

nectar - a sweet liquid made by plants, usually to attract insects, birds, bats, and other pollinators.

parched - become very dry from wind or lack of water.

pollen - small powdery grains from a flower that fertilize the female part of a plant to make seeds.

pollinate - to carry pollen from one plant to another so new plants can develop.

pounce - to jump on and hold.

roost - to rest on a branch, or perch.

savanna - a flat grassland with few trees.

spore - a single plant cell that can grow into a new plant.

shallow - not deep; close to the surface of the ground.

spine - the sharp, needle-like part of a plant or animal, found on cacti and porcupines.

twilight - the time just before nightfall.

Index